THIS BOOK BELONGS TO:
....

THANK YOU FOR CHOOSING US
TRY OUR OTHER COLORING BOOKS ON AMAZON

- Lily Ann Coloring Book -

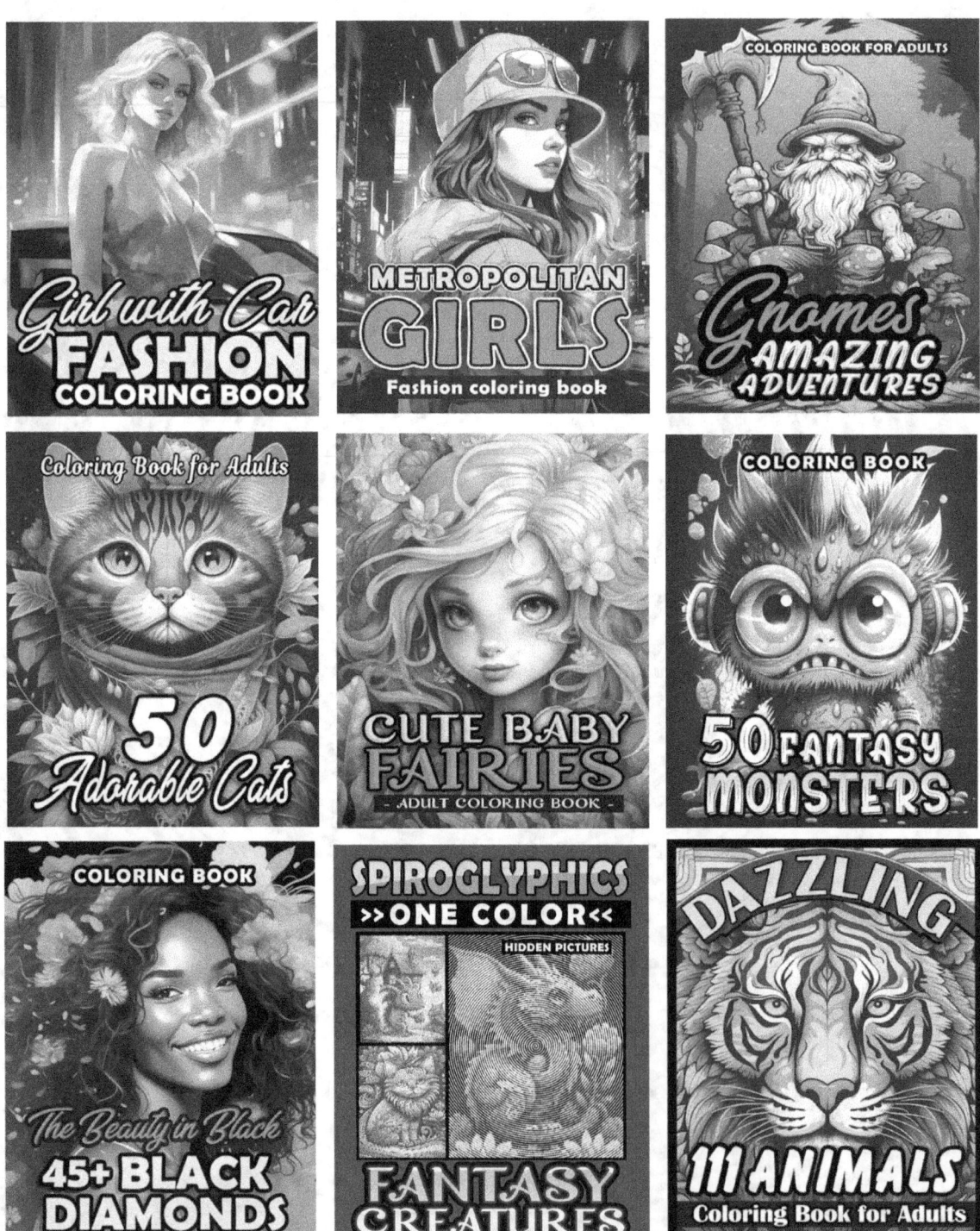

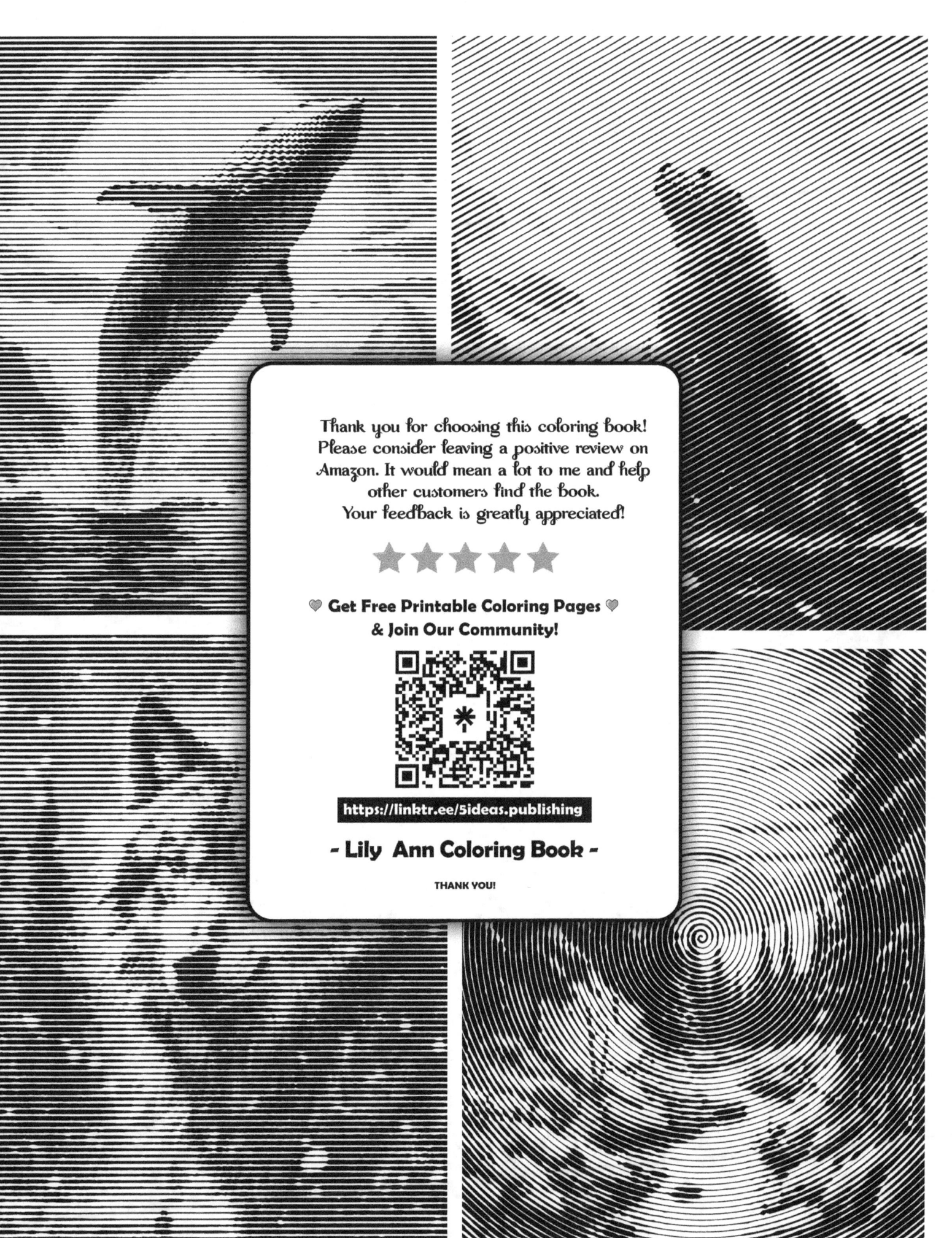

Thank you for choosing this coloring book!
Please consider leaving a positive review on
Amazon. It would mean a lot to me and help
other customers find the book.
Your feedback is greatly appreciated!

♡ **Get Free Printable Coloring Pages** ♡
& Join Our Community!

https://linktr.ee/5ideas.publishing

- Lily Ann Coloring Book -

THANK YOU!

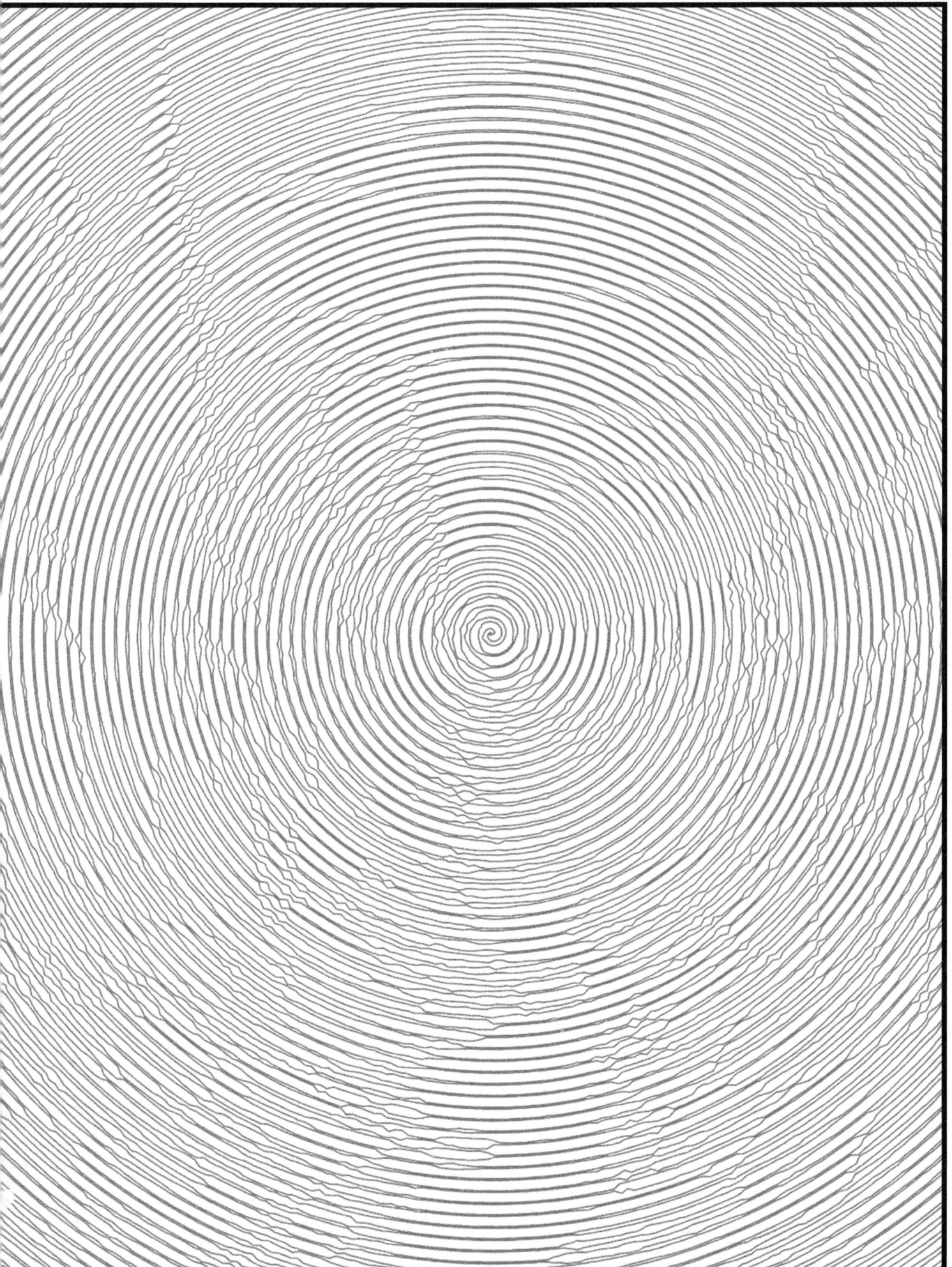

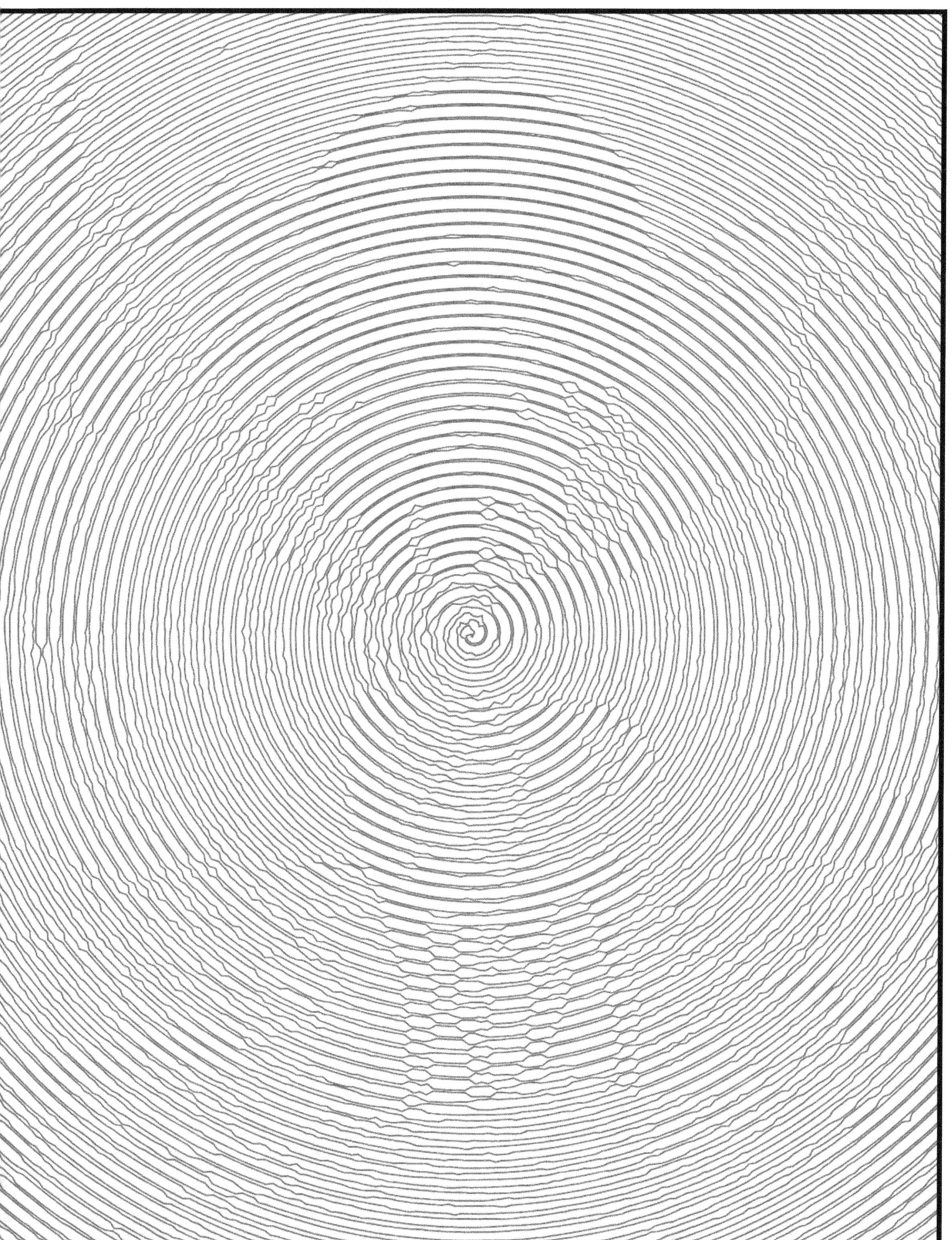

LILY ANN
COLORING BOOK

LILY ANN
COLORING BOOK

LILY ANN
COLORING BOOK

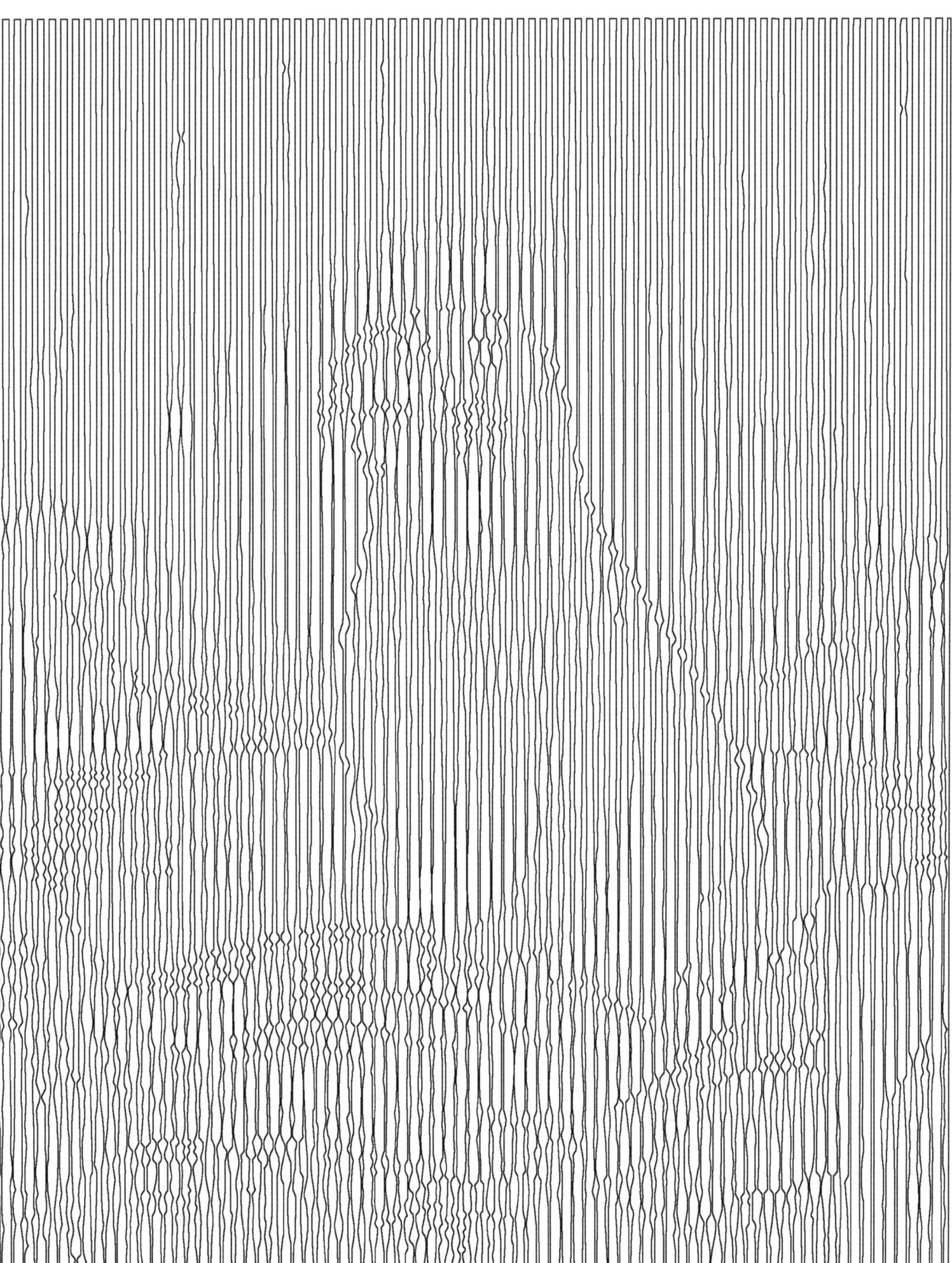

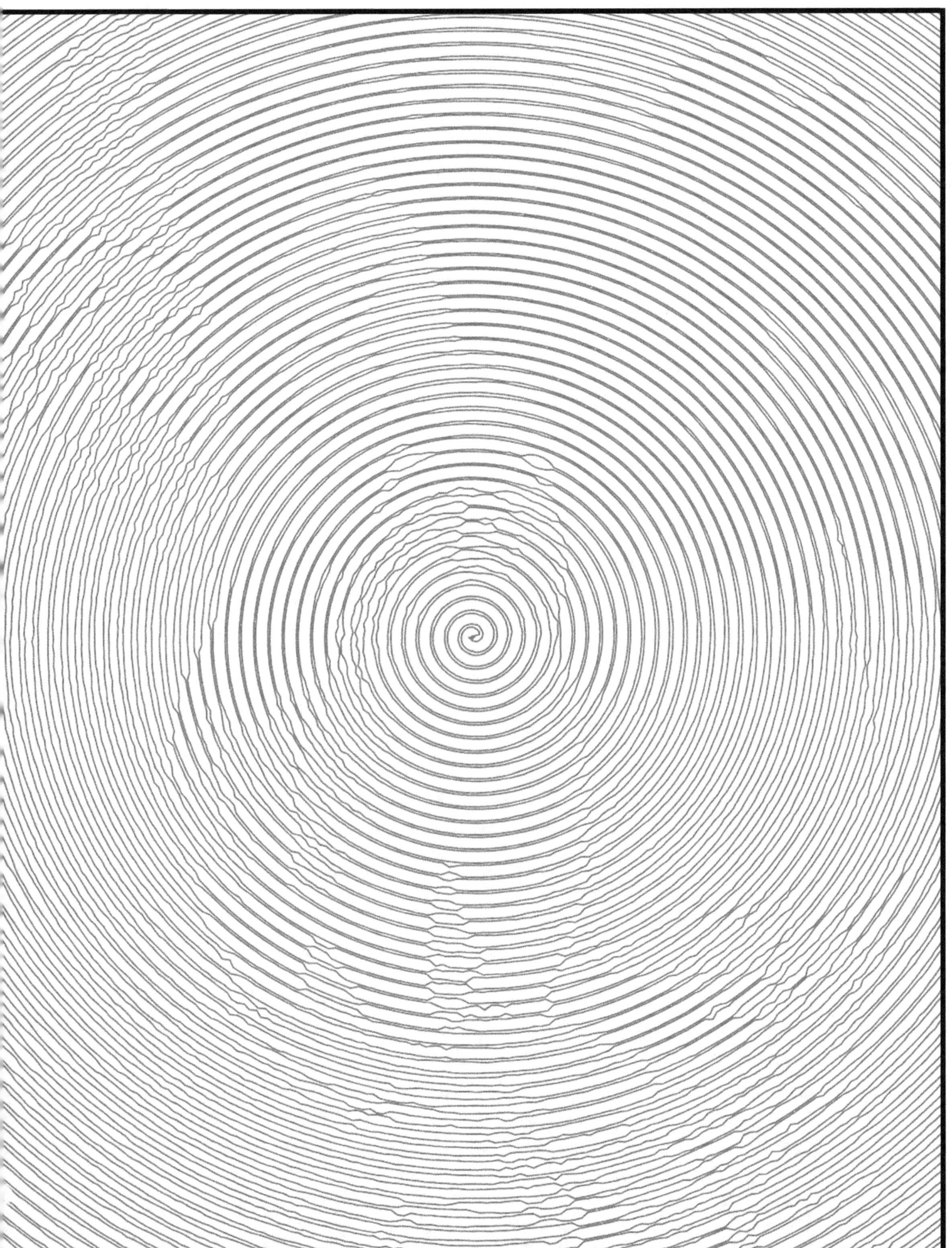

LILY ANN
COLORING BOOK

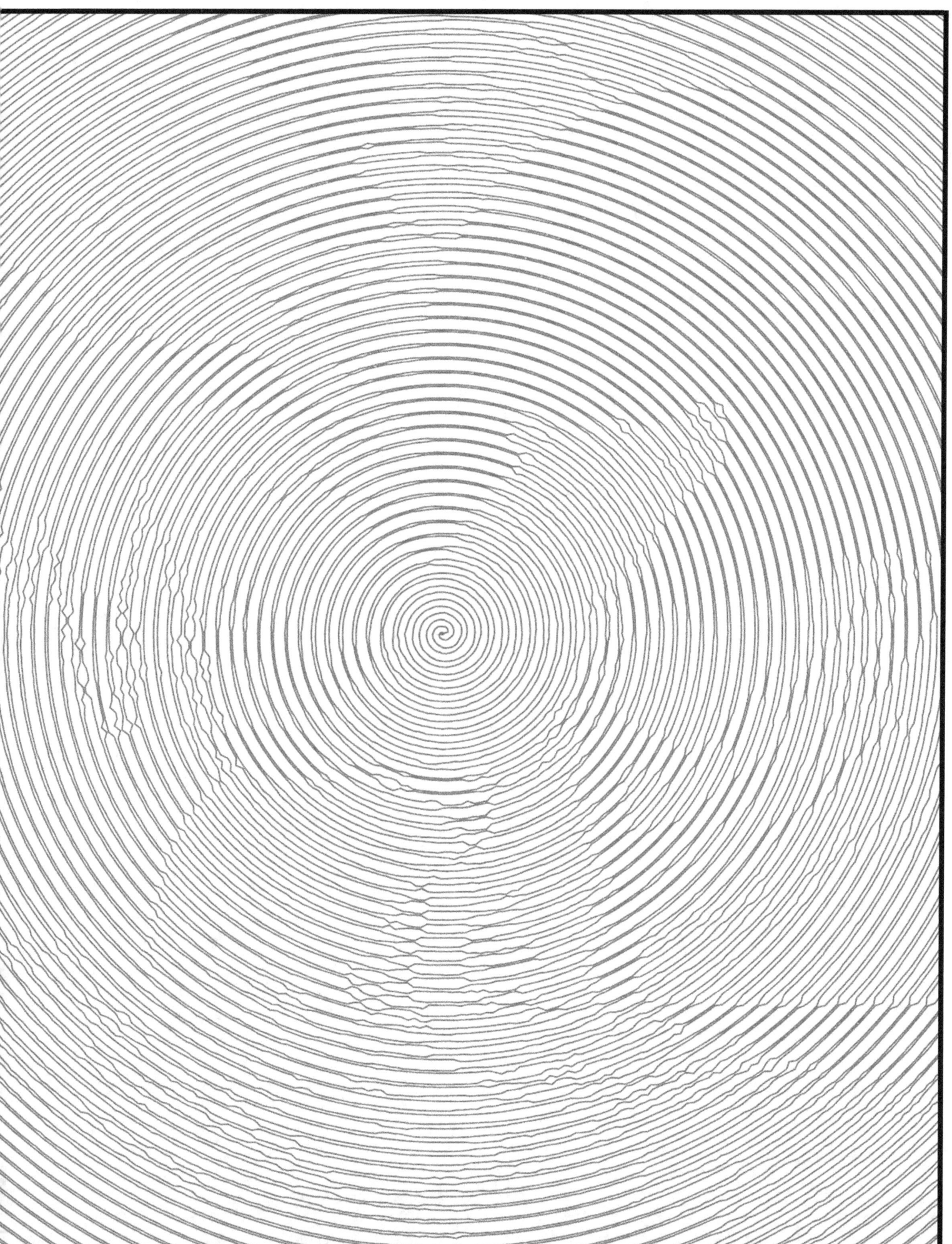

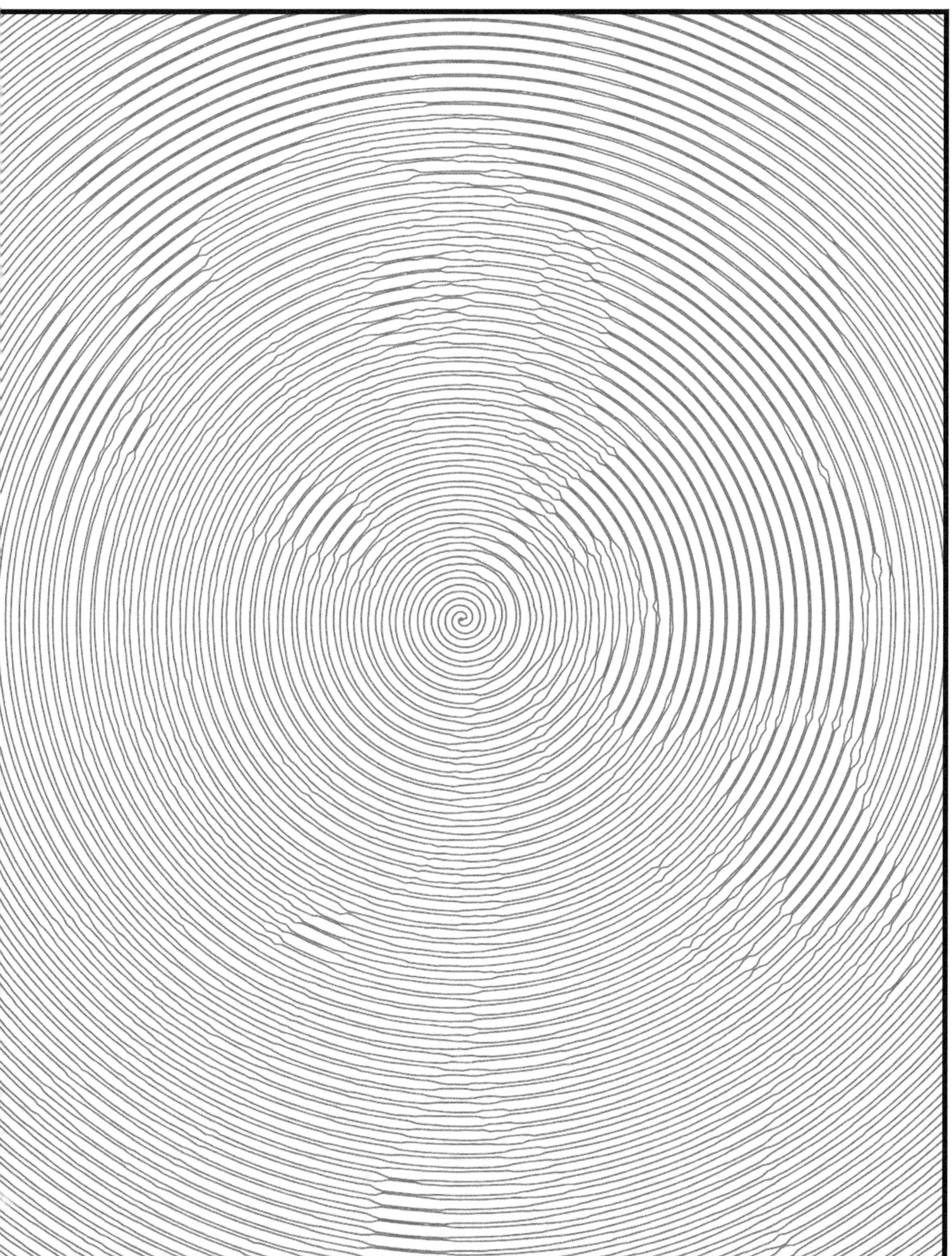

LILY ANN
COLORING BOOK

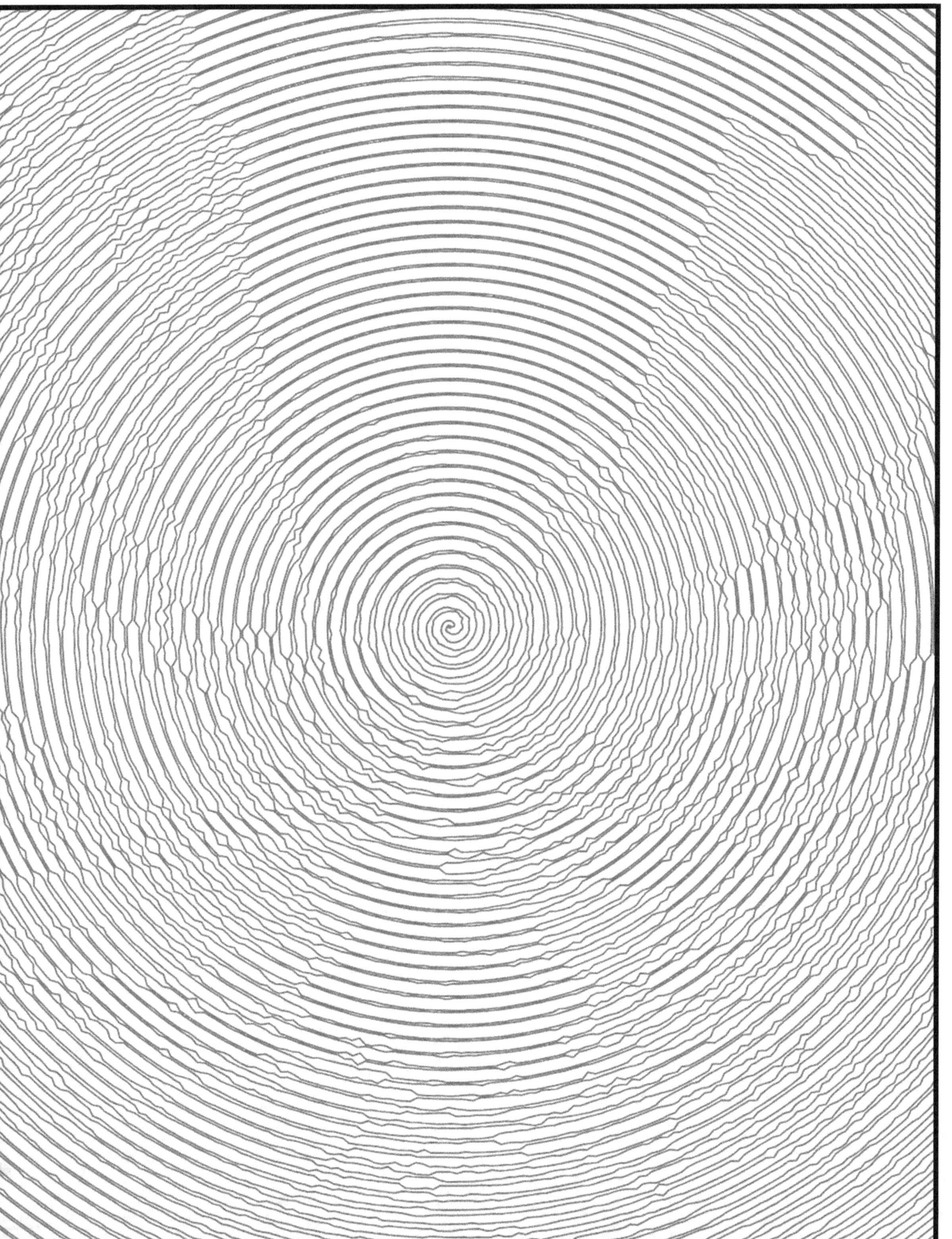

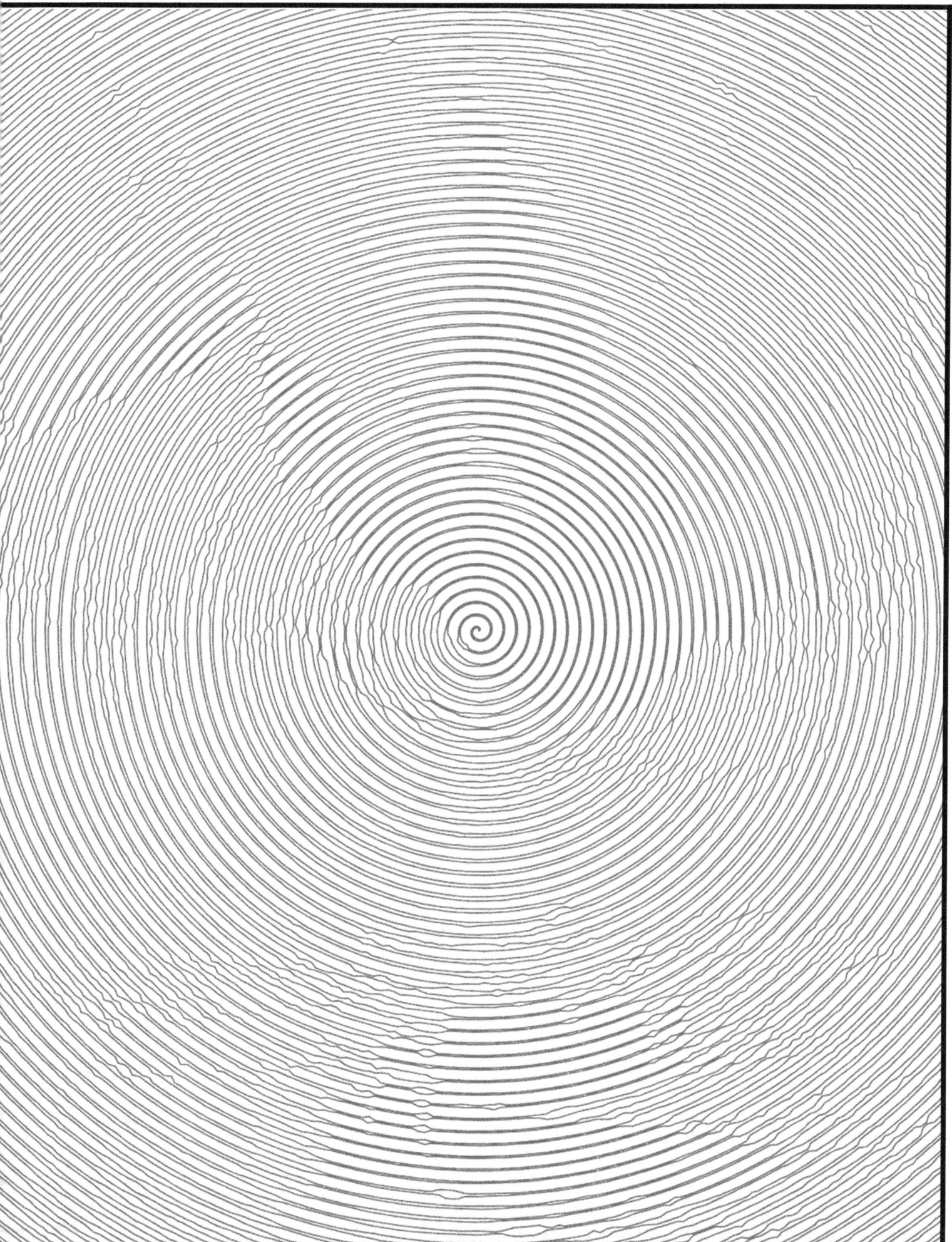

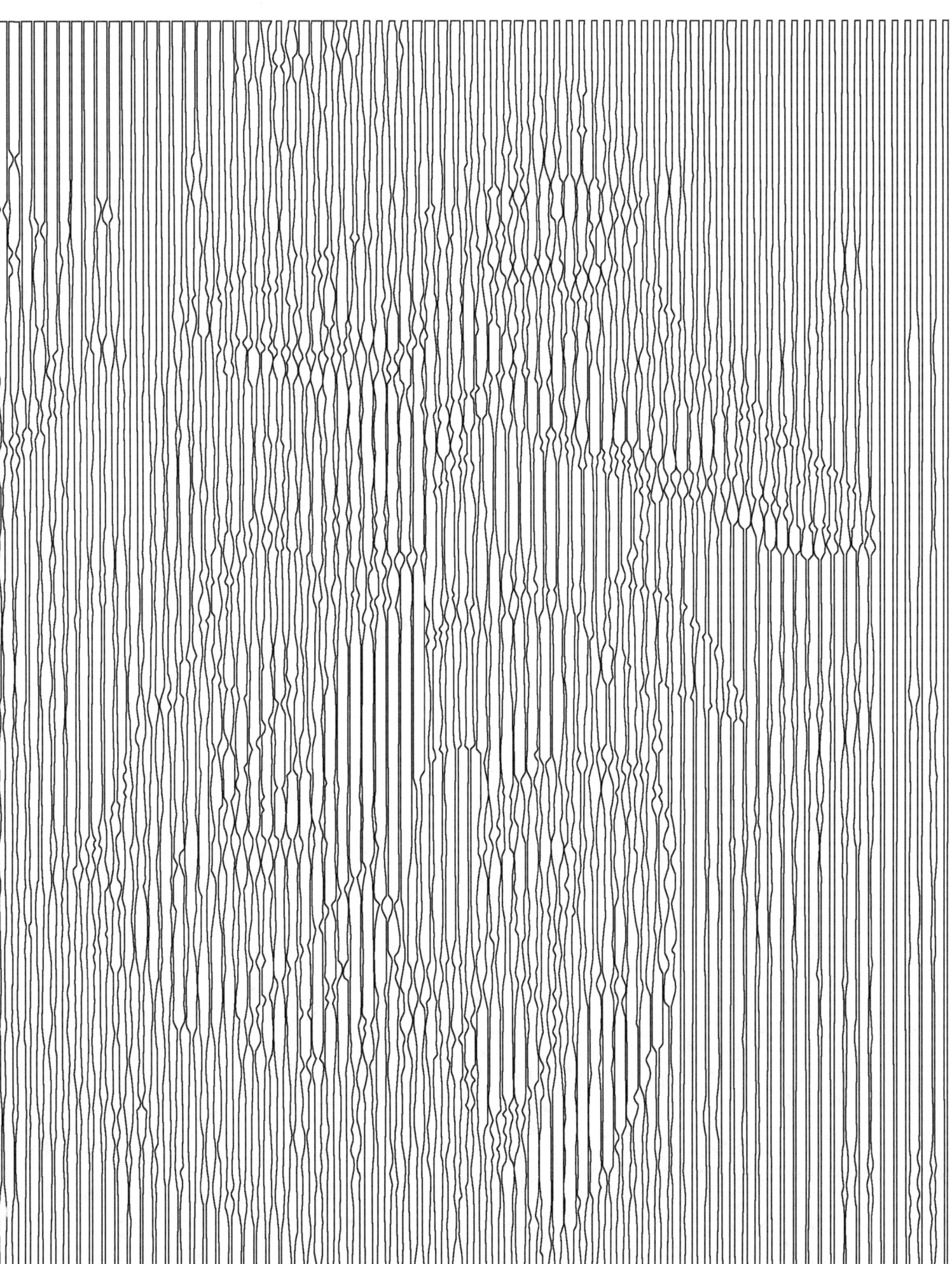

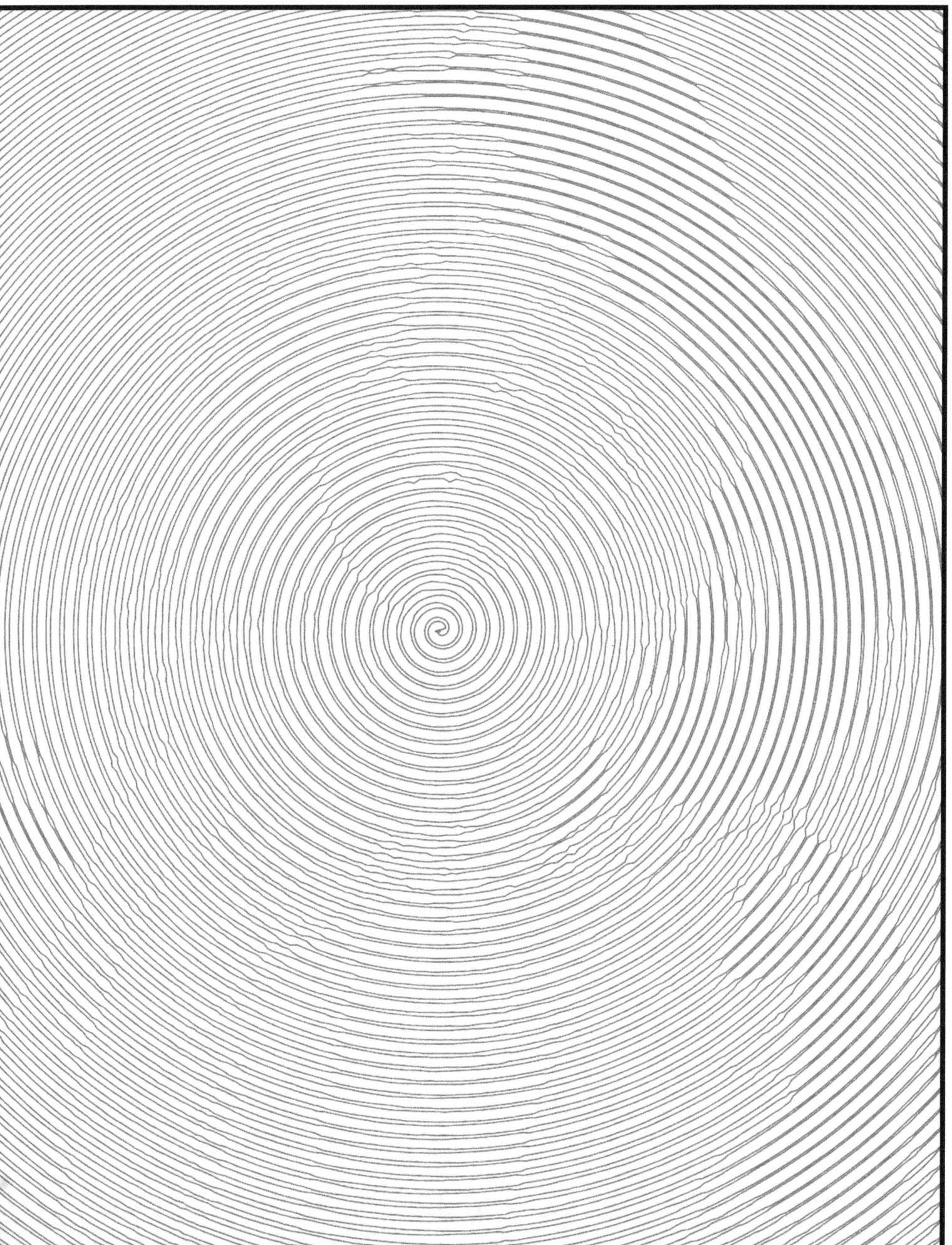

LILY ANN
COLORING BOOK

LILY ANN
COLORING BOOK

LILY ANN
COLORING BOOK

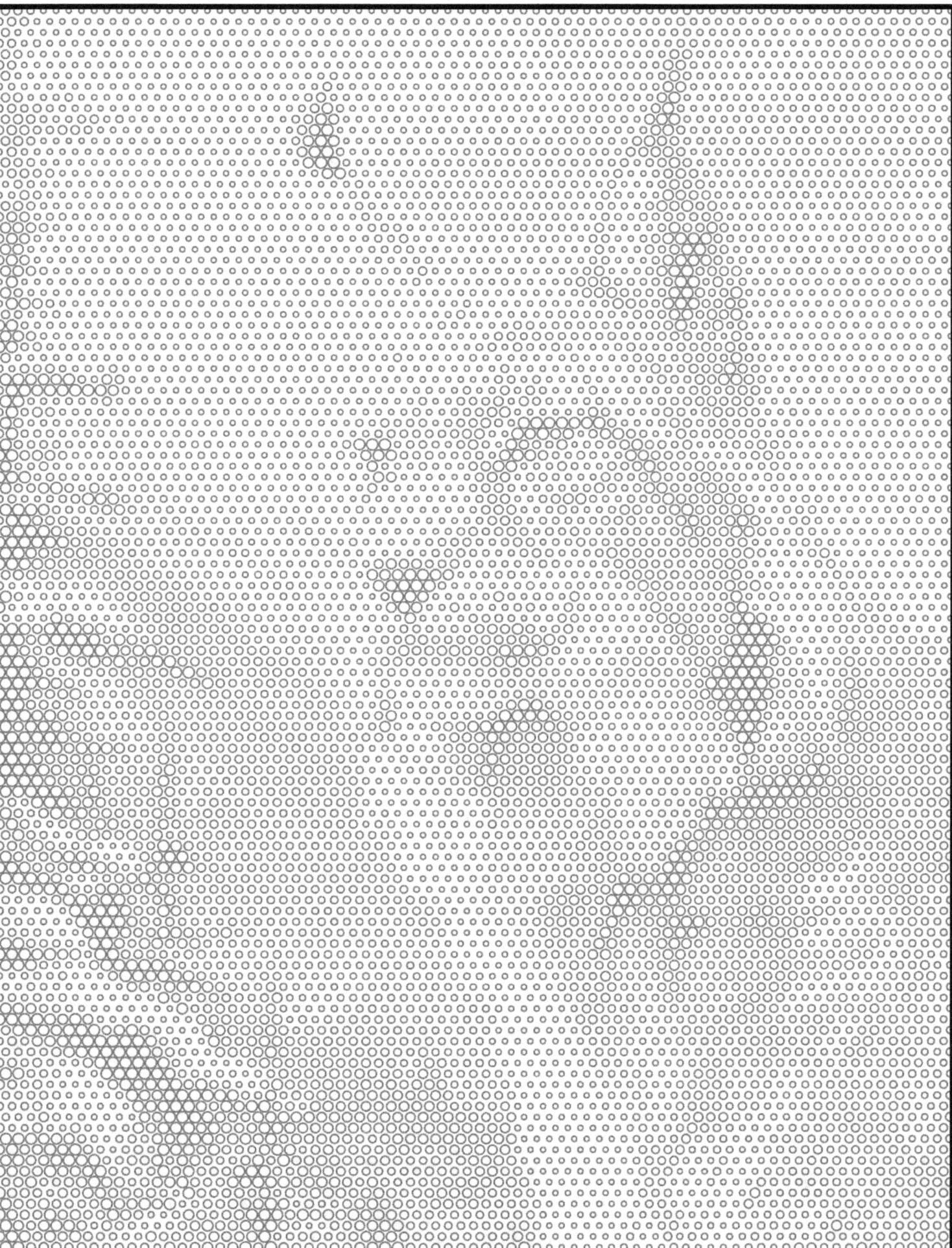

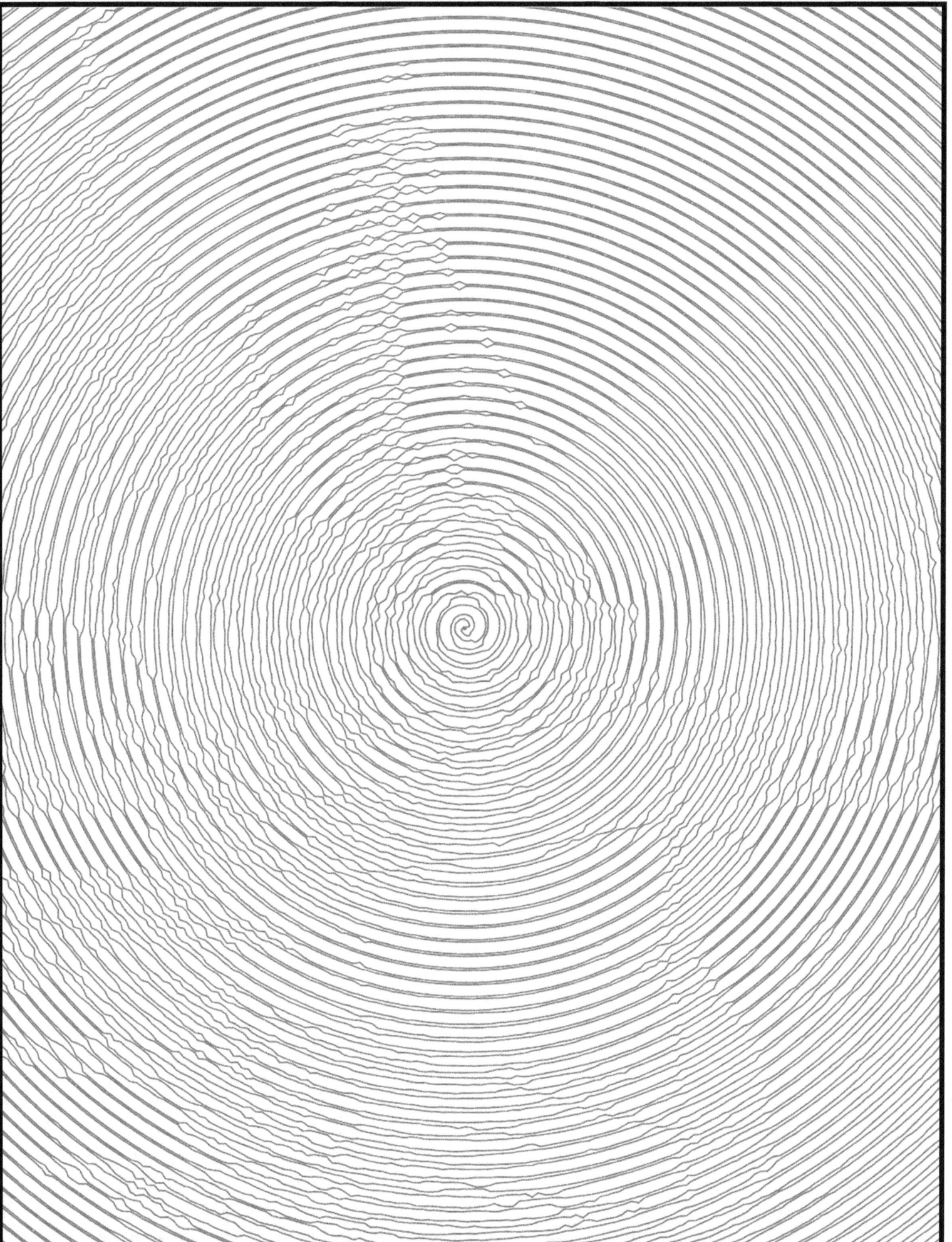

LILY ANN
COLORING BOOK

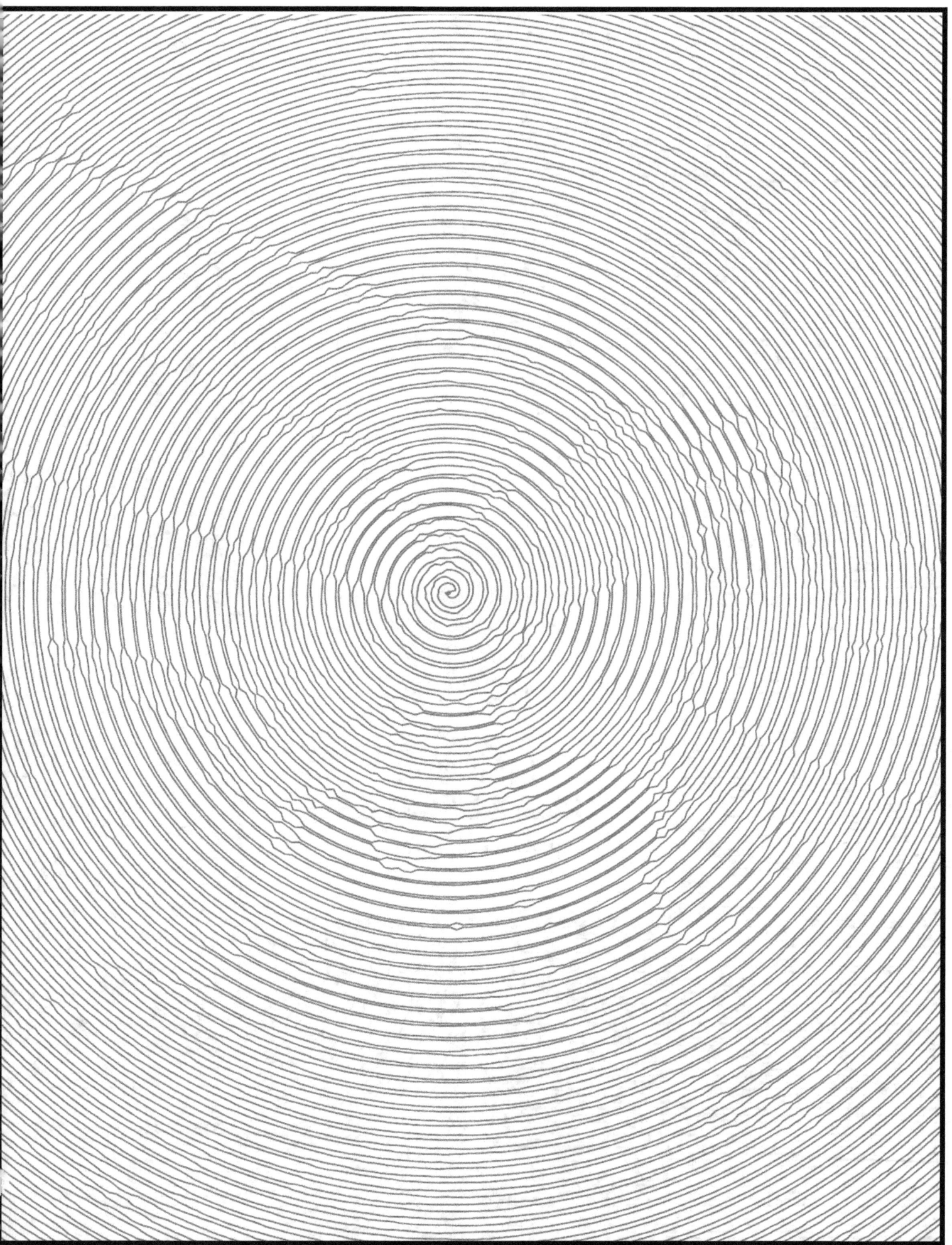

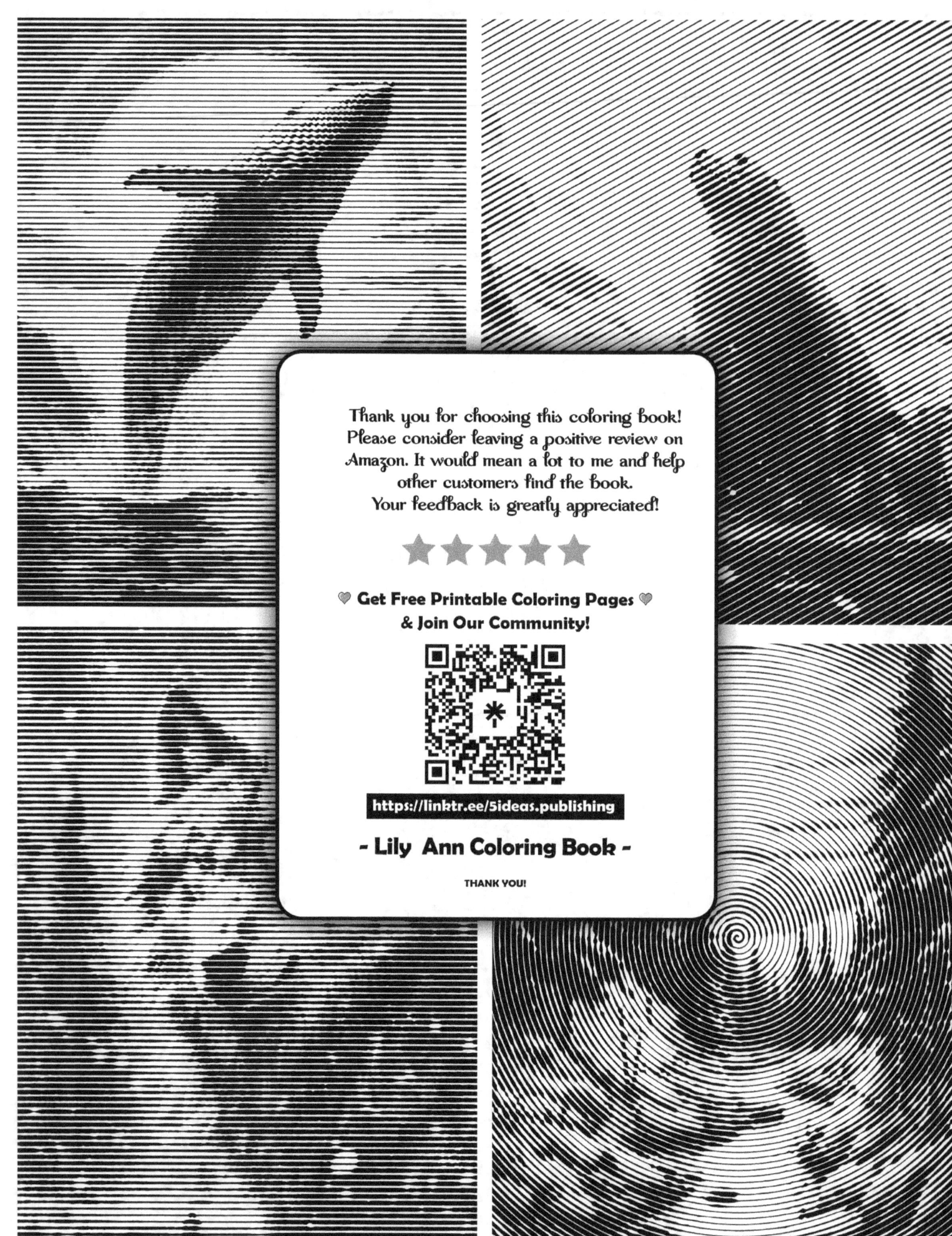

Thank you for choosing this coloring book!
Please consider leaving a positive review on
Amazon. It would mean a lot to me and help
other customers find the book.
Your feedback is greatly appreciated!

♡ **Get Free Printable Coloring Pages** ♡
& Join Our Community!

https://linktr.ee/5ideas.publishing

- Lily Ann Coloring Book -

THANK YOU!

THANK YOU FOR CHOOSING US
TRY OUR OTHER COLORING BOOKS ON AMAZON

- Lily Ann Coloring Book -

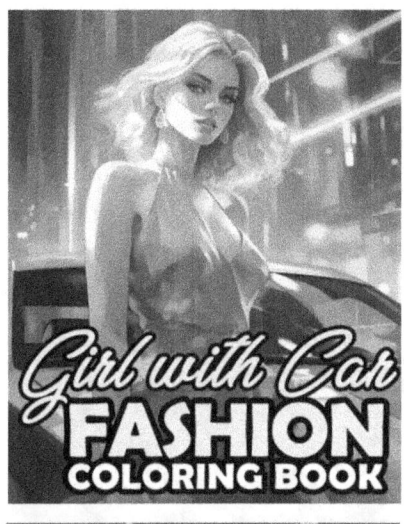

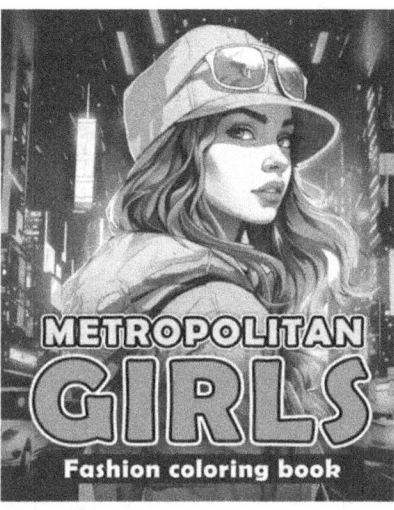

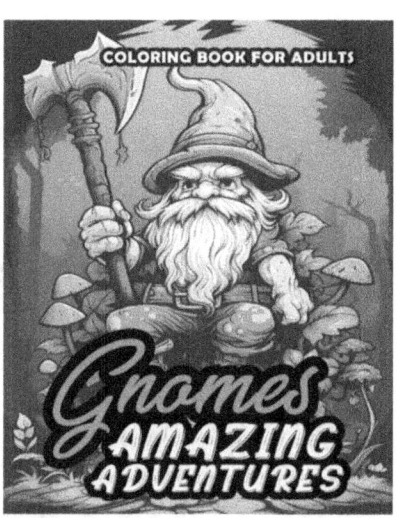

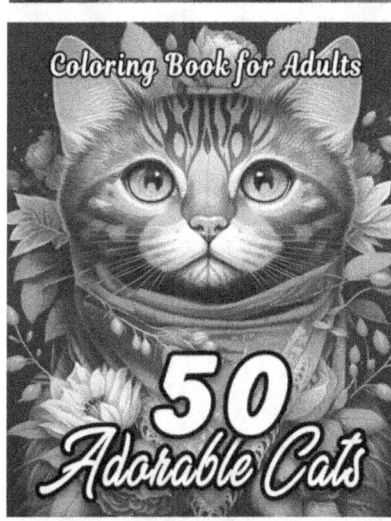

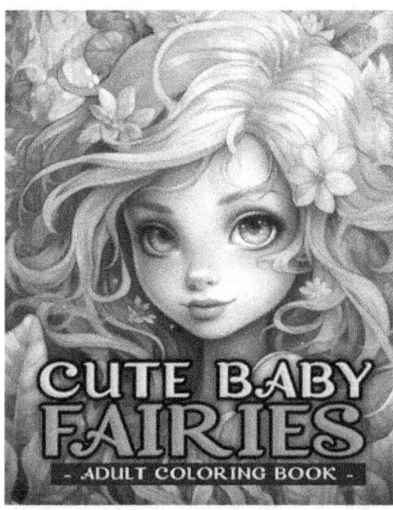

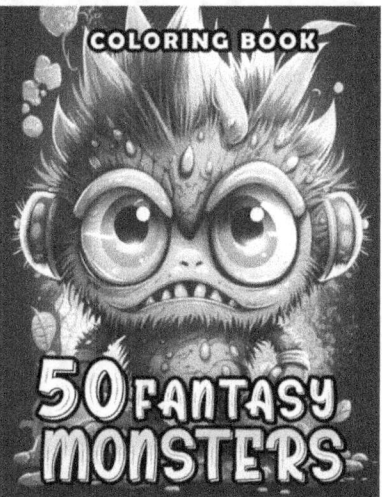

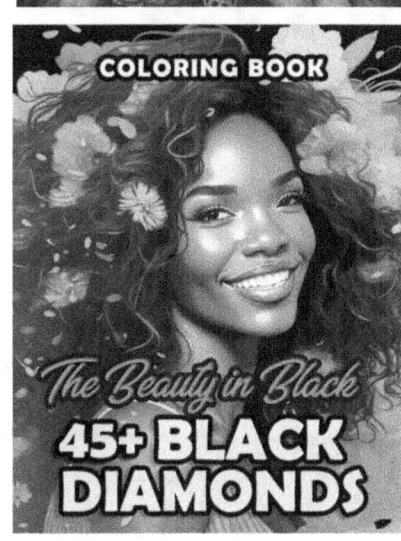

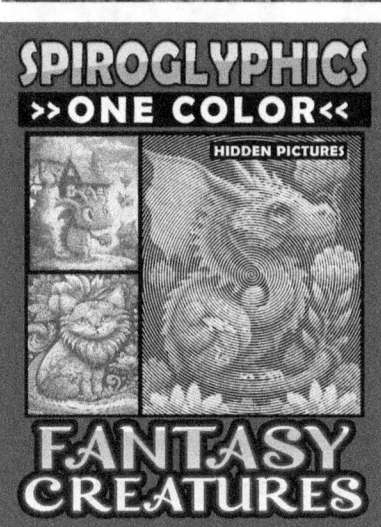

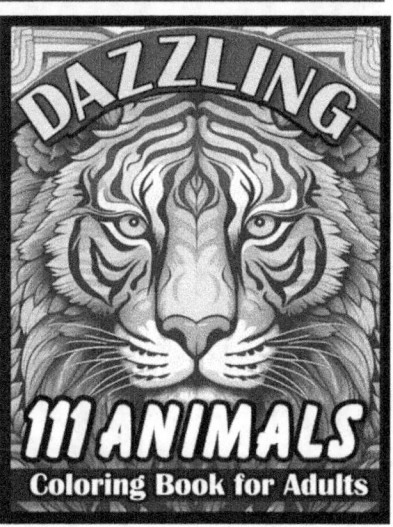